# Magna Carta

# for Know-It-Alls

**Filiquarian Publishing, LLC.**

Filiquarian Publishing, LLC is publishing this edition of Magna Carta for Know-It-Alls, due to its status under the GNU Free Documentation License.

The cover of Magna Carta for Know-It-Alls, and "For Know-It-Alls" imprint is copyright 2008, Filiquarian Publishing, LLC.

Magna Carta for Know-It-Alls is available for free pdf download at www.know-it-alls.com/dbooks/M082

**Filiquarian Publishing, LLC.**

# Magna Carta

# for Know-It-Alls

Magna Carta (Latin for "Great Charter", literally "Great Paper"), also called Magna Carta Libertatum ("Great Charter of Freedoms"), is an English charter originally issued in 1215. Magna Carta was the most significant early influence on the extensive historical process that led to the rule of constitutional law today. Magna Carta influenced the development of the common law and many constitutional documents, such as the United States Constitution and Bill of Rights, and is considered one of the most important legal documents in the history of democracy.

Magna Carta was originally written because of disagreements among Pope Innocent III, King John and the English barons about the rights of the King. Magna Carta required the King to renounce certain rights, respect certain legal procedures and accept that his will could be bound by the law. It explicitly protected certain rights of the King's subjects, whether free or fettered — most notably the writ of habeas corpus, allowing appeal against unlawful imprisonment. Many clauses were renewed throughout the Middle Ages, and further during the Tudor and Stuart periods, and the 18th century. By the late 19th century, most clauses in their original form had been repealed from English law.

There are some popular misconceptions about Magna Carta, such as that it was the first document to limit the power of an English King by law, that it in practice limited the power of the king, and that it is a single static document. In fact it was not the first (it was partly based on the Charter of Liberties); it mostly did not limit the power of the King in the Middle Ages; and it is a collection of documents referred to under a common name.

## Background

After the Norman conquest of England in 1066 and advances in the 12th century, the English king had by 1199 become a powerful and influential monarch in Europe. Factors contributing to this include the sophisticated centralised government created by the procedures of the new Anglo-Saxon systems of governance[clarify]; and extensive Anglo-Norman land holdings in Normandy. But after King John of England was crowned in the early 13th century, a series of failures at home and abroad, combined with perceived abuses of the king's power, led the English barons to revolt and attempt to restrain what the king could legally do.

## France

King John's actions in France were a major cause of discontent in the realm. At the time of his accession to the throne after Richard's death, there were no set rules to define the line of succession. King John, as Richard's younger brother, was crowned over Richard's nephew, Arthur of Brittany. Since Arthur still had a claim over the Anjou empire, however, John needed the approval of the French king, Philip Augustus. To get it, John gave to Philip large tracts of the French-speaking Anjou territories.

When John later married Isabella of Angoulême, her previous fiancé (Hugh IX of Lusignan, one of John's vassals) appealed to Philip, who then declared forfeit all of John's French lands, including the rich Normandy. Philip declared Arthur as the true ruler of the Anjou throne and invaded John's French holdings in mid-1202 to give it to him. John had to act to save face, but his eventual actions did not achieve this—he ended up killing Arthur in suspicious circumstances, thus losing the little support he had from his French barons.

After the defeat of John's allies at the Battle of Bouvines, Philip retained all of John's northern French territories, including Normandy (although Aquitaine remained in English hands for a time). These serious military defeats, which lost to the English a major source of income, made John unpopular at home. Worse, to recoup his expenses, he had to further tax the already unhappy barons.

## The Church

At the time of John's reign there was still a great deal of controversy as to how the Archbishop of

Canterbury was to be elected, although it had
become traditional that the monarch would
appoint a candidate with the approval of the
monks of Canterbury.

But in the early 13th century, the bishops began to
want a say. To retain control, the monks elected
one of their numbers to the rôle. But John,
incensed at his lack of involvement in the
proceedings, sent John de Gray, the Bishop of
Norwich, to Rome as his choice. Pope Innocent III
declared both choices invalid and persuaded the
monks to elect Stephen Langton. Nevertheless,
John refused to accept this choice and exiled the
monks from the realm. Infuriated, Innocent
ordered an interdict (prevention of public worship
— mass, marriages, the ringing of church bells,
etc.) in England in 1208, excommunicated John in
1209, and encouraged Philip to invade England in
1212.

John finally backed down and agreed to endorse
Langton and allow the exiles to return. To
completely placate the pope, he gave England and
Ireland as papal territories and rented them back as
a fiefdom for 1,000 marks per annum. This

surrender of autonomy to a foreign power further enraged the barons.

## Taxes

King John needed money for armies, but the loss of the French territories, especially Normandy, greatly reduced the state income, and a huge tax would have to be raised in order to attempt to reclaim these territories. Yet, it was difficult to raise taxes because of the tradition of keeping them at the same level.

Novel efforts to raise income included a Forest law, a set of regulations about the king's forest, which were easily broken and severely punished. John also increased the pre-existing scutage (feudal payment to an overlord replacing direct military service) eleven times in his seventeen years as king, as compared to eleven times in twice that period covering three monarchs before him. The last two of these increases were double the increase of their predecessors. He also imposed the first income tax, which raised what was, at the time, the extortionate sum of £70,000.

## Rebellion and Signing of the Document

By 1215, some of the most important barons in England had had enough, and they entered London in force on June 10, 1215, with the city showing its sympathy with their cause by opening its gates to them. They, and many of the moderates not in overt rebellion, forced King John to agree to the "Articles of the Barons", to which his Great Seal was attached in the meadow at Runnymede on June 15, 1215. In return, the barons renewed their oaths of fealty to King John on June 19, 1215. A formal document to record the agreement was created by the royal chancery on July 15: this was the original Magna Carta. An unknown number of copies of it were sent out to officials, such as royal sheriffs and bishops.

The most significant clause for King John at the time was clause 61, known as the "security clause", the longest portion of the document. This established a committee of 25 barons who could at any time meet and overrule the will of the King, through force by seizing his castles and possessions if needed. This was based on a medieval legal practice known as distraint, but it was the first time it had been applied to a monarch. In addition, the King was to take an oath of loyalty to the committee.

Clause 61 essentially neutered John's power as a monarch, making him King in name only. He renounced it as soon as the barons left London, plunging England into a civil war, called the First Barons' War. Pope Innocent III also annulled the "shameful and demeaning agreement, forced upon the King by violence and fear." He rejected any call for restraints on the King, saying it impaired John's dignity. He saw it as an affront to the Church's authority over the King and the 'papal territories' of England and Ireland, and he released John from his oath to obey it.

## Magna Carta Re-Issued

John died during the war, from dysentery, on October 18, 1216, and this quickly changed the nature of the war. His nine-year-old son, Henry III, was next in line for the throne. The royalists believed the rebel barons would find the idea of loyalty to the child Henry more palatable, so the boy was swiftly crowned in late October 1216, and the war ended.

Henry's regents reissued Magna Carta in his name on November 12, 1216, omitting some clauses, such as clause 61, and again in 1217. When he turned 18 in 1225, Henry III reissued Magna Carta, this time in a shorter version with only 37 articles.

Henry III ruled for 56 years (the longest reign of an English Monarch in the Medieval period) so that by the time of his death in 1272, Magna Carta had become a settled part of English legal precedent.

Henry III's son and heir Edward I's Parliament reissued Magna Carta for the final time on October 12, 1297, as part of a statute called Confirmatio cartarum, reconfirming Henry III's shorter version of Magna Carta from 1225.

## Content

Magna Carta was originally written in Latin. A large part of Magna Carta was copied, nearly verbatim, from the Charter of Liberties of Henry I, issued when Henry I ascended to the throne in 1100, which bound the king to certain laws regarding the treatment of church officials and nobles, effectively granting certain civil liberties to the church and the English nobility.

The document commonly known as Magna Carta today is not the 1215 charter but a later charter of 1225, and is usually shown in the form of The Charter of 1297 when it was confirmed by Edward I. At the time of the 1215 charter, many of the provisions were not meant to make long term changes but simply to right the immediate wrongs, and therefore The Charter was reissued three times in the reign of Henry III (1216, 1217 and 1225) in order to provide for an updated version. After this, each individual king for the next two hundred years (until Henry V in 1416) personally confirmed the 1225 charter in his own charter.

## Rights Still in Force Today

For modern times, the most enduring legacy of Magna Carta is considered the right of habeas corpus. This right arises from what are now known as clauses 36, 38, 39, and 40 of the 1215 Magna Carta.

Three clauses of the 1297 version of Magna Carta remain in legal force in England and Wales. Clause 1 guarantees the freedom of the English Church. Although this originally meant freedom from the King, later in history it was used for different purposes (see below). Clause 9 guarantees the "ancient liberties" of the City of London. Clause 29 guarantees a right to due process.

* I. FIRST, We have granted to God, and by this our present Charter have confirmed, for Us and our Heirs for ever, that the Church of England shall be free, and shall have all her whole Rights and Liberties inviolable. We have granted also, and given to all the Freemen of our Realm, for Us and our Heirs for ever, these Liberties underwritten, to have and to hold to them and their Heirs, of Us and our Heirs for ever.

* IX. THE City of London shall have all the old Liberties and Customs which it hath been used to have. Moreover We will and grant, that all other

Cities, Boroughs, Towns, and the Barons of the Five Ports, and all other Ports, shall have all their Liberties and free Customs.

* XXIX. NO Freeman shall be taken or imprisoned, or be disseised of his Freehold, or Liberties, or free Customs, or be outlawed, or exiled, or any other wise destroyed; nor will We not pass upon him, nor condemn him, but by lawful judgment of his Peers, or by the Law of the Land. We will sell to no man, we will not deny or defer to any man either Justice or Right.[1]

The repeal of clause 26 in 1829 [2] was the first time a clause of Magna Carta was repealed. With the document's perceived protected status broken, in 150 years nearly the whole charter was repealed, leaving just Clauses 1, 9, and 29 still in force after 1969. Most of it was repealed in England and Wales by the Statute Law Revision Act 1863, and in Ireland by the Statute Law (Ireland) Revision Act 1872.[1]

# Feudal Rights Still in Place in 1225

Several clauses were present in the 1225 charter but are no longer in force and would have no real place in the post-feudal world. Clauses 2 to 7 refer to the feudal death duties; defining the amounts and what to do if an heir to a fiefdom is underage or is a widow. Clause 23 provides no town or person should be forced to build a bridge across a river. Clause 33 demands the removal of all fish weirs. Clause 43 gives special provision for tax on reverted estates and Clause 44 states that forest law should only apply to those in the king's forest.

## Feudal Rrights Not in the 1225 Charter

Some provisions have no bearing in the world today, since they are feudal rights and were not even included in the 1225 charter. Clauses 9 to 12, 14 to 16, and 25 to 26 deal with debt and taxes and Clause 27 with intestacy.

The other clauses state that no one may seize land in debt except as a last resort; that underage heirs and widows should not pay interest on inherited loans; that county rents will stay at their ancient amounts; and that the crown may only seize the value owed in payment of a debt, that aid (taxes for warfare or other emergency) must be reasonable, and that scutage (literally, shield-payment, payment in lieu of actual military service used to finance warfare) may only be sought with the consent of the kingdom.

Clause 14 states that the common consent of the kingdom was to be sought from a council of the archbishops, bishops, earls and greater Barons. This later became the great council, which led to the first parliament

## Judicial Rights

Clauses 17 to 22 allowed for a fixed law court, which became the chancellery, and defines the scope and frequency of county assizes. They also state that fines should be proportionate to the offence, that they should not be influenced by ecclesiastical property in clergy trials, and that their peers should try people. Many think that this gave rise to jury and magistrate trial, but its only manifestation in the modern world was the right of a lord to a criminal trial in the House of Lords at first instance (abolished in 1948).

Clause 24 states that crown officials (such as sheriffs) may not try a crime in place of a judge. Clause 34 forbids repossession without a writ precipe. Clauses 36 to 38 state that writs for loss of life or limb are to be free, that someone may use reasonable force to secure their own land, and that no one can be tried on their own testimony alone.

Clauses 36, 38, 39 and 40 collectively define the right of Habeas Corpus. Clause 36 requires courts to make inquiries as to the whereabouts of a prisoner, and to do so without charging any fee. Clause 38 requires more than the mere word of an official, before any person could be put on trial. Clause 39 gives the courts exclusive rights to punish anyone. Clause 40 disallows the selling or the delay of justice. Clauses 36 and 38 were removed from the 1225 version, but were reinstated in later versions. The right of Habeas Corpus as such was first invoked in court in the year 1305.

Clause 54 says that no man may be imprisoned on the testimony of a woman except on the death of her husband.

## Anti-Corruption and Fair Trade

Clauses 28 to 32 state that no royal officer may take any commodity such as grain, wood or transport without payment or consent or force a knight to pay for something the knight could do himself, and that the king must return any lands confiscated from a felon within a year and a day.

Clause 35 sets out a list of standard measures, and Clauses 41 and 42 guarantee the safety and right of entry and exit of foreign merchants.

Clause 45 says that the King should only appoint royal officers where they are suitable for the post.

Clause 46 provides for the guardianship of monasteries.

# Temporary Provisions

Some provisions were for immediate effect and were not in any later charter. Clauses 47 and 48 abolish most of Forest Law (these were later taken out of Magna Carta and formed into a separate charter, the Charter of the Forests)[3]. Clauses 49, 52 to 53 and 55 to 59 provide for the return of hostages, land and fines taken in John's reign.

Article 50 states that no member of the D'Athèe family may be a royal officer. Article 51 calls for all foreign knights and mercenaries to leave the realm.

Articles 60, 62 and 63 provide for the application and observation of the Charter and say that the Charter is binding on the King and his heirs forever, but this was soon deemed dependent on each succeeding king reaffirming the Charter under his own seal.

# Great Council

The first long-term constitutional effect arose from
Clauses 14 and 61, which permitted a council
composed of the most powerful men in the
country to exist for the benefit of the state rather
than in allegiance to the monarch. Members of the
council were also allowed to renounce their oath
of allegiance to the King in pressing
circumstances and to pledge allegiance to the
council and not to the King in certain instances.
The common council was responsible for taxation,
and although it was not representative, its
members were bound by decisions made in their
absence. The common council, later called the
Great Council, was England's proto-parliament.

The Great Council only existed to give input on
the opinion of the kingdom as a whole, and it only
had power to control scutage until 1258 when
Henry III got into debt fighting in Sicily for the
pope. The barons agreed to a tax in exchange for
reform, leading to the Provisions of Oxford. But
Henry got a papal bull allowing him to set aside
the provisions and in 1262 told royal officers to

ignore the provisions and only to obey Magna Carta. The barons revolted and seized the Tower of London, the Cinque ports and Gloucester. Initially the King surrendered, but when Louis IX of France arbitrated in favour of Henry, Henry crushed the rebellion. Later he ceded somewhat, passing the Statute of Marlborough in 1267, which allowed writs for breaches of Magna Carta to be free of charge, enabling anyone to have standing to apply the Charter.

This secured the position of the Great Council forever, but its powers were still very limited. The council originally only met three times per year and so was subservient to the King's council, Curiae Regis, who, unlike the Great Council, followed the king wherever he went.

Still, in some senses the council was an early form of parliament. It had the power to meet outside the authority of the King and was not appointed by him. While executive government descends from the Curiae Regis, parliament descends from the Great Council, which was later called the parliamentum. However, the Great Council was very different from modern parliament. There were no knights, let alone commons, and it was composed of the most powerful men, rather than elected citizens.

Magna Carta had little effect on subsequent development of parliament until the Tudor period. Knights and count representatives attended the Great Council (Simon de Montfort's Parliament), and the council became far more representative under the model parliament of Edward I which included two knights from each county, two burgesses from each borough and two citizens from each city. The Commons separated from the Lords in 1341. The right of the Commons to exclusively sanction taxes (based on a withdrawn provision of Magna Carta) was re-asserted in 1407, although it was not in force in this period. The power vested in the Great Council by, albeit withdrawn, Clause 14 of Magna Carta became vested in the House of Commons but Magna Carta was all but forgotten for about a century, until the Tudors.

# Tudor Dynasty

The Magna Carta was the first entry on the statute books, but after 1472, it was not mentioned for a period of nearly 100 years. There was much ignorance about the document. The few who did know about the document spoke of a good king being forced by an unstable pope and rebellious barons "to attaine the shadow of seeming liberties" and that it was a product of a wrongful rebellion against the one true authority, the king. The original Magna Carta was seen as an ancient document with shadowy origins and as having no bearing on the Tudor world. Shakespeare's King John makes no mention of the Charter at all but focuses on the murder of Arthur. The Charter in the statute books was thought to have arisen from the reign of Henry III.

## First Uses of the Charter as a Bill of Rights

This statute was used widely in the reign of Henry VIII but was seen as no more special than any other statute and could be amended and removed. But later in the reign, the Lord Treasurer stated in

the Star Chamber that many had lost their lives in
the Baronial wars fighting for the liberties which
were guaranteed by the Charter, and therefore it
should not so easily be overlooked as a simple and
regular statute.

The church often attempted to invoke the first
clause of the Charter to protect itself from the
attacks by Henry, but this claim was given no
credence. Francis Bacon was the first to try to use
Clause 39 to guarantee due process in a trial.

Although there was a re-awakening of the use of
Magna Carta in common law, it was not seen (as it
was later) as an entrenched set of liberties
guaranteed for the people against the Crown and
Government. Rather, it was a normal statute,
which gave a certain level of liberties, most of
which could not be relied on, least of all against
the king. Therefore, the Charter had little effect on
the governance of the early Tudor period.
Although lay parliament evolved from the Charter,
by this stage the powers of parliament had
managed to exceed those humble beginnings. The
Charter had no real effect until the Elizabethan
age.

# Reinterpretation of the Charter

In the Elizabethan age, England was becoming a powerful force in Europe. In academia, earnest but futile attempts were made to prove that Parliament had Roman origins. The events at Runnymede in 1215 were "re-discovered", allowing a possibility to show the antiquity of Parliament, and Magna Carta became synonymous with the idea of an ancient house with origins in Roman government.

The Charter was interpreted as an attempt to return to a pre-Norman state of things. The Tudors saw the Charter as proof that their state of governance had existed since time immemorial and the Normans had been a brief break from this liberty and democracy. This claim is disputed in certain circles but explains how Magna Carta came to be regarded as such an important document.

Magna Carta again occupied legal minds, and it again began to shape how that government was run. Soon the Charter was seen as an immutable entity. In the trial of Arthur Hall for questioning the antiquity of the House, one of his alleged crimes was an attack on Magna Carta.

## Edward Coke's Opinions

One of the first respected jurists to write seriously about the great charter was Edward Coke, who had a great deal to say on the subject and was influential in the way Magna Carta was perceived throughout the Tudor and Stuart periods, although his opinions changed across time and his writing in the Stuart period was more influential. In the Elizabethan period, Coke wrote of Parliament evolving alongside the monarchy and not existing by any allowance on the part of the monarch. However he was still fiercely loyal to Elizabeth, and the monarchy still judged the Charter in the same light it always had: an evil document forced out of their forefathers by brute force. He therefore prevented a re-affirmation of the charter from passing the House, and although he spoke highly of the charter, he did not speak out against imprisonments without due process. This came back to haunt him later when he moved for a reaffirmation of the charter.

Coke was not alone in his confused opinions about the charter among the people in that era. The Petition of Right in 1628 was meant as a reaffirmation of the charter but was defeated by the Attorney General (Robert Heath). He stated that the petition claimed it was a mere codification of existing law stemming from Magna Carta, but, he claimed, there was no precedent shown as to these laws existing in such as a way as they bound the present king; there was a definite feeling that the king could not be bound by law and therefore Clause 39 and all others did not apply to him. The charter was seen as important as a statement as to the antiquity of Parliament, that it was pre-Norman, and not because it was the catalyst to the genesis of Parliament. Again, certain modern critics dispute this latter point. The Charter was seen in part as entrenched law by Coke's opinion and no one would dare deny it, but it was not seen as binding on the king. Such suggestions were impermissible until the Stuart period.

## Magna Carta's Tole in the Lead-up to the Civil War

By the time of the Stuarts, Magna Carta had attained an almost mythical status for its admirers and was seen as representing a 'golden age' of English liberties extant prior to the Norman invasion. Whether or not this 'golden age' ever truly existed is open to debate; regardless, proponents of its application to English law saw themselves as leading England back to a pre-Norman state of affairs. What is true, however is that this age existed in the hearts and minds of people of the time. Magna Carta was not important because of the liberties it bestowed, but simply as 'proof' of what had come before; many great minds influentially exalted the Charter; by the seventeenth century, Coke was talking of the Charter as an indispensable method of limiting the powers of the Crown, a popular principle in the Stuart period where the kings were proclaiming their divine right and were looking, in the minds of some of their subjects, towards becoming absolute monarchs.

It was not the content of the Charter which has made it so important in the history of England, but more how it has been perceived in the popular mind. This is something that certainly started in the Stuart period, as the Charter represented many things, which are not to be found in the Charter itself. Firstly it was used to claim liberties against the Government in general rather than just the Crown and the officers of the crown, secondly that it represented that the laws and liberties of England, specifically Parliament, dated back to a time immemorial and thirdly, that it was not only just but right to usurp a king who disobeyed the law.

For the last of these reasons Magna Carta began to represent a danger to the monarchy; Elizabeth ordered that John Coke stop a bill from going through Parliament which would have reaffirmed the validity of the Charter, and Charles I ordered the suppression of a book which Coke intended to write on Magna Carta. The powers of Parliament were growing, and on Coke's death, parliament ordered his house to be searched; the manuscripts were recovered, and the book was published in 1642 (at the end of Charles I's Personal Rule).

Parliament began to see Magna Carta as its best way of claiming supremacy over the crown and began to state that they were the sworn defenders of the liberties — fundamental and immemorial — which were to be found in the Charter.

In the four centuries since the Charter had originally catered for their creation, Parliament's power had increased greatly from their original level where they existed only for the purpose that the king had to seek their permission in order to raise scutage. They had become the only body allowed to raise tax, a right which although descended from the 1215 Great Charter was not guaranteed by it, since it was removed from the 1225 edition. Parliament had become so powerful that the Charter was being used both by those wishing to limit Parliament's power (as a new organ of the Crown), and by those who wished Parliament to rival the king's power (as a set of principles Parliament was sworn to defend against the king). When it became obvious that some people wished to limit the power of Parliament by claiming it to be tantamount to the crown, Parliament claimed they had the sole right of interpretation of the Charter.

This was an important step; for the first time Parliament was claiming itself a body as above the law; whereas one of the fundamental principles in English law was that the law, Parliament, the monarch, and the church held all, albeit to different extents. Parliament was claiming exactly what Magna Carta wanted to prevent the king from claiming, a claim of not being subject to any higher form of power. This was not claimed until ten years after the death of Lord Coke, but he would not have agreed with this, because he claimed in the English Constitution the law was supreme and all bodies of government were subservient to the supreme law, which is to say the common law, as embodied in the Great Charter. These early discussions of Parliament sovereignty seemed to only involve the Charter as the entrenched law, and the discussions were simply about whether Parliament had enough power to repeal the document.

Although it was important for Parliament to be able to claim themselves more powerful than the King in the forthcoming struggle, the Charter provided for this very provision. Clause 61 of the

Charter enables people to swear allegiance to what became the Great Council and later Parliament and therefore to renounce allegiance to the king. Moreover, Clause 61 allowed for the seizing of the kingdom by the body which later became Parliament if Magna Carta was not respected by the king or Lord Chief Justice. So there was no need to show any novel level of power in order to overthrow the king; it had already been set out in Magna Carta nearly half a millennium before. Parliament was not ready to repeal the Charter yet however, and in fact, it was cited as the reason why ship money was illegal (the first time Parliament overruled the king).

## Trial of Archbishop Laud

Further proof of the significance of Magna Carta is shown in the trial of Archbishop Laud in 1645. Laud was tried with attempting to subvert the laws of England including writing a condemnation of Magna Carta claiming that as the Charter came about due to rebellion it was not valid (a widely held opinion less than a century before, when the 'true' Magna Carta was thought to be the 1225 edition, with the 1215 edition being considered less valid for this very reason). However, Laud was not trying to say that Magna Carta was evil, and he actually used the document in his defence. He claimed his trial was against the right of the freedom of the church (as the Bishops were voted out of Parliament in order to allow for parliamentary condemnation of him) and, that he was not given the benefit of due process contrary to Clauses 1 and 39 of the Charter. By this stage, Magna Carta had passed a great distance beyond the original intentions for the document, and the Great Council had evolved beyond a body merely ensuring the application of the Charter. It had gotten to the stage where the Great Council or Parliament was inseparable from the ideas of the Crown as described in the Charter and therefore it was potentially not just the King that was bound by the Charter, but Parliament also.

## Civil War and Interregnum

After seven years of civil war, the king surrendered and was executed; it seemed Magna Carta no longer applied, as there was no King. Oliver Cromwell was accused of destroying Magna Carta, and many thought he should be crowned just so that it would apply. Cromwell had much disdain for the Magna Carta, at one point describing it as "Magna Farta" to a defendant who sought to rely on it[4].

In this time of foment, there were many revolutionary theorists, and many based their theories at least initially on Magna Carta, in the misguided belief that Magna Carta guaranteed liberty and equality for all.

## Levellers

The Levellers believed that all should be equal and free without distinction of class or status. They believed that Magna Carta was the 'political bible', which should be prized above any other law and that it could not be repealed. They prized it so highly that they believed all (such as Archbishop Laud) who "trod Magna Carta…under their feet" deserved to be attacked at all levels. The original idea was to achieve this through Parliament but there was little support, because at the time the Parliament was seeking to impose itself as above Magna Carta. The Levellers claimed Magna Carta was above any branch of government, and this led to the upper echelons of the Leveller movement denouncing Parliament. They claimed that Parliament's primary purpose was not to rule the people directly but to protect the people from the extremes of the King; they claimed that Magna Carta adequately did this and therefore Parliament should be subservient to it.

After the Civil War, Cromwell refused to support the Levellers and was denounced as a traitor to Magna Carta. The importance of Magna Carta was greatly magnified in the eyes of the Levellers. John Lilburne, one of the leaders of the movement, was known for his great advocacy of the Charter and was often known to explain its purpose to lay people and to expose the misspeaking against it in the popular press of the time. He was quoted as saying the ground and foundation of my freedome I build upon the grand charter of England. However, as it became apparent that Magna Carta did not grant the level of liberty demanded by the Levellers, the movement reduced its advocacy of it. Welwyn, another leader of the movement, advocated natural law and other doctrines as the primary principles of the movement. This was mainly because the obvious intention of Magna Carta was to grant rights only to the barons and the episcopacy, and not the general and egalitarian rights the Levellers were claiming. Also influential, however, was Spelman's rediscovery of the existence of the feudal system at the time of Magna Carta, which seemed to have less and less effect on the world of the time. The only right, which the Levellers could trace back to 1215, possibly prized over all others, was the right to due process granted by Clause 39. One thing the Levellers did agree on with the popular beliefs of the time was that Magna Carta was an attempt to return to the fabled pre-Norman 'golden age'.

## Diggers

However, not all such groups advocated Magna Carta. The Diggers were a very early socialistic group who called for all land to be available to all for farming and the like. Gerrard Winstanley, a leader of the group, despised Magna Carta as a show of the hypocrisy of the post-Norman law, since Parliament and the courts advocated Magna Carta and yet did not even follow it themselves. The Diggers did, however, believe in the pre-

Norman golden age and wished to return to it, and they called for the abolition of all Norman and post-Norman law.

## Charles II

The Commonwealth was relatively short lived however, and when Charles II took the throne in 1660, he vowed to respect both the common law and the Charter. Parliament was established as the everyday government of Britain, independent of the King but not more powerful. However, the struggles based on the Charter were far from over and took on the form of the struggle for supremacy between the two Houses of Parliament.

## Within Parliament

In 1664, the British navy seized Dutch lands in both Africa and America leading to full-scale war with Holland in 1665. The Lord Chancellor Edward Lord Clarendon, resisted an alliance with the Spanish and Swedes in favour of maintaining a relationship with the French, who were the allies of the Dutch. This lack of a coherent policy led to the Second Anglo-Dutch War (1665-67), with the

Dutch burning ships in the docks at Chatham, and the blame was placed on Clarendon. The Commons demanded that Clarendon be indicted before the Lords, but the Lords refused, citing the due process requirements of the Charter, giving Clarendon the time to escape to Europe.

A very similar set of events followed in 1678 when the Commons asked the Lords to indict Thomas Lord Danby on a charge of fraternising with the French. As with Clarendon the Lords refused, again citing Magna Carta and their own supremacy as the upper house. Before the quarrel could be resolved, Charles dissolved the Parliament. When Parliament was re-seated in 1681, again the Commons attempted to force an indictment in the Lords. This time Edward Fitzharris who was accused of writing libellously that the King was involved in a papist plot with the French (including the overthrowing of Magna Carta). However, the Lords doubted the veracity of the claim and refused to try Fitzharris saying Magna Carta stated that everyone must be subject to due process and therefore he must be tried in a lower court first. This time the Commons retorted that it was the Lords who were denying justice under Clause 39 and that the Commons were right to cite the Charter as their precedent. Again, before any true conclusions could be drawn Charles dissolved the Parliament, although more to serve his own ends and to rid himself of a predominantly Whig Parliament, and Fitzharris was tried in a regular court (the King's Bench) and executed for treason. Here the Charter, once again, was used far beyond the content of its provisions, and simply being used as a representation of justice. Each house was claiming the Charter under Clause 39 supported its supremacy, but the power of the King was still too great for either house to come out fully as the more powerful.

## Outside Parliament

The squabble also continued outside the Palace of Westminster. In 1667 the Lord Chief Justice and important member of the House of Lords, Lord Keating, forced a grand jury of Middlesex to return a verdict of murder when they wanted to return one of manslaughter. However, his biggest crime in the eyes of the Commons was that, when the jury objected on the grounds of Magna Carta, he scoffed and exclaimed "Magna Carta, what ado with this have we?" The Commons were incensed at this abuse of the Charter and accused him of "endangering the liberties of the people". However, the Lords claimed he was just referring to the inappropriateness of the Charter in this context, but Keating apologised anyway. In 1681 the next Lord Chief Justice, Lord Scroggs, was condemned by the Commons first for being too severe in the so-called 'papist plot trials' and second for dismissing another Middlesex grand jury in order to secure against the indictment of the Duke of York, the Catholic younger brother of the King later to become James II. Charles again dissolved Parliament before the Commons could impeach Scroggs, and removed him from office on a good pension. Just as it seemed that the Commons might be able to impose their supremacy over the Lords, the King intervened and proved he was still the most powerful force in the government. However, it was certainly beginning to become established that the Commons were the primary branch of Government, and they used the Charter as much as they could in order to achieve this end.

## Supremacy of the Commons

This was not the end of the struggle however, and in 1679 the Commons passed the Habeas Corpus Act of 1679, which greatly reduced the powers of the Crown. The act passed through the Lords by a small majority, arguably establishing the Commons as the more powerful House. This was the first time since the importance of the Charter had been so magnified that the Government had admitted that the liberties granted by the Charter were inadequate. However, this did not completely oust the position of the Charter as a symbol of the law of the 'golden age' and the basis of common law.

It did not take long before the questioning of the Charter really took off and Sir Matthew Hale soon afterwards introduced a new doctrine of common law based on the principle that the Crown (including the government cabinet in that definition) made all law and could only be bound by the law of God, and showed that the 1215 charter was effectively overruled by the 1225 charter, further undermining the idea that the charter was unassailable, adding credence to the idea that the Commons were a supreme branch of Government. Some completely denied the relevance of the 1215 Charter as it was forced upon the King by rebellion (although the fact that the 1225 charter was forced on a boy by his guardians was overlooked). It was similarly argued against the Charter that it was nothing more than a relaxation of the rigid feudal laws and therefore had no meaning outside of that application.

## Glorious Revolution

The danger posed by the fact that Charles II had no legitimate child was becoming more and more real, as this meant that the heir apparent was the Duke of York, a Catholic and firm believer in the divine right of kings, threatening the establishment of the Commons as the most powerful arm of government. Parliament did all it could to prevent James's succession but was prevented when Charles dissolved the Parliament. In February 1685, Charles died of a stroke and James II assumed the throne of the United Kingdom. Almost straight away James attempted to impose

Catholicism as the religion of the country and to regain the royal prerogative now vested in the Parliament. Parliament was slightly placated when James's four-year-old son died in 1677 and it seemed his Protestant daughter Mary would take his throne. However when James' second wife, Mary of Modena, gave birth to a male heir in 1688 Parliament could not take the risk that another Catholic monarch would assume the throne and take away their power, and in 1688 the Convention Parliament declared that James had broken the contract of Magna Carta and nullified his claim to the throne. This finally proved that Parliament was the major power in the British Government; Mary, James II's eldest daughter was invited to take the throne with her husband William of Orange. Many thought that, with bringing in a new monarch, it would be prudent to define what powers this monarch should have, so the Bill of Rights was created. The Bill of Rights went far beyond what the Magna Carta had ever set out to achieve. It stated that the Crown could not make law without Parliament. Although the raising of taxes was specifically mentioned, it did not limit itself to such, as Magna Carta did. However, one important thing to note is that the writers of the Bill did not seem to think that the Bill included any new provisions of law; all the powers it 'removes' from the crown it refers to as 'pretended' powers, insinuating that the rights of Parliament listed in the Bill already existed under a different authority, presumably Magna Carta. So the importance of Magna Carta was not completely extinguished at this point, although it was somewhat diminished.

## Eighteenth Century

The power of the Magna Carta myth still existed in the 18th century; in 1700 Samuel Johnson talked of Magna Carta being "born with a grey beard" referring to the belief that the liberties set out in the Charter harked back to the Golden Age and time immemorial. However, ideas about the nature of law in general were beginning to change. In 1716 the Septennial Act was passed, which had a number of consequences. Firstly, it showed that Parliament no longer considered its previous statutes unassailable, as this act provided that the parliamentary term was to be seven years, whereas fewer than twenty-five years had passed since the Triennial Act (1694), which provided that a parliamentary term was to be three years. It also greatly extended the powers of Parliament. Previously, all legislation that passed in a parliamentary session had to be listed in the election manifesto, so in effect the electorate was consulted on all issues that were to be brought before Parliament. However, with a seven-year term, it was unlikely, if not impossible, that all the legislation passed would be discussed at the election. This gave Parliament the freedom to legislate as it liked during its term. This was not Parliamentary sovereignty as understood today however, as although Parliament could overrule its own statutes, it was still considered itself bound by the higher law, such as Magna Carta. Arguments for Parliamentary sovereignty were not new; however, even its proponents would not have expected Parliament to be as powerful as it is today. For example, in the previous century, Coke had discussed how Parliament might well have the power to repeal the common law and Magna Carta, but they were, in practice, prohibited from doing so, as the common law and Magna Carta were so important in the constitution that it would be dangerous to the continuing existence of the constitution to ever repeal them.

# Extent of the Commons' Powers

In 1722 the Bishop of Rochester (Francis
Atterbury (a Stuart Jacobite)), a member of the
House of Lords, was accused of treason. The
Commons locked him in the Tower of London,
and introduced a bill intending to remove him
from his post and send him into exile. This, once
again, brought up the subject of which was the
more powerful house, and exactly how far that
power went. Atterbury claimed, and many agreed,
that the Commons had no dominion over the
Lords. Other influential people disagreed
however; for example, the Bishop of Salisbury
(also a Lord) was of the strong opinion that the
powers of Parliament, mainly vested in the
Commons, were sovereign and unlimited and
therefore there could be no limit on those powers
at all, implying the dominion of the lower house
over the upper house. Many intellectuals agreed;
Jonathan Swift went so far as to say that
Parliament's powers extended to altering or
repealing Magna Carta. This claim was still
controversial, and the argument incensed the
Tories. Bolingbroke spoke of the day when

"liberty is restored and the radiant volume of Magna Carta is returned to its former position of Glory". This belief was anchored in the relatively new theory that when William the Conqueror invaded England he only conquered the throne, not the land, and he therefore assumed the same position in law as the Saxon rulers before him. The Charter was therefore a recapitulation or codification of these laws rather than (as previously believed) an attempt to reinstate these laws after the tyrannical Norman Kings. This implied that these rights had existed constantly from the 'golden age immemorial' and could never be removed by any government. The Whigs on the other hand claimed that the Charter only benefited the nobility and the church and granted nowhere near the liberty they had come to expect. However although the Whigs attacked the content of the Charter, they did not actually attack the myth of the 'golden age' or attempt to say that the Charter could be repealed, and the myth remained as immutable as ever.

## America

The 1765 Stamp Act extended the stamp duty, which had been in force on home territory since 1694 to cover the American colonies as well. However, the colonists despised this since they were not represented in Parliament and refused to see how a body, which did not represent them, could tax them. The cry 'no taxation without representation' rang throughout the colonies.

The influence of Magna Carta can be clearly seen in the U.S. Bill of Rights, which enumerates various rights of the people and restrictions on government power, such as:

No person shall be ... deprived of life, liberty, or property, without due process of law.

Article 21 from the Declaration of Rights in the Maryland Constitution of 1776 reads:

That no freeman ought to be taken, or imprisoned, or disseized of his freehold, liberties, or privileges, or outlawed, or exiled, or in any manner destroyed, or deprived of his life, liberty, or property, but by the judgment of his peers, or by the law of the land.

## Parliamentary Sovereignty

The doctrine of parliamentary supremacy (if not parliamentary sovereignty) had largely been established 1765 when William Blackstone argued strongly for sovereignty in his Commentaries on the English Law. He essentially argued that absolute supremacy must exist in one of the arms of Government; and he thought it resided in Parliament, as Parliament could legislate on anything, even legislating the impossible if they wished, regardless of whether it was practical. The debate over whether or not Parliament could limit or overrule the supposed rights granted by Magna Carta was to prove to be the basis for the discussion over parliamentary sovereignty. Blackstone thought however that despite Parliament's power, it should respect Magna Carta as a show of law from time immemorial. The other great legal mind of the time Jeremy Bentham used the Charter to attack legal abuses.

# John Wilkes

In 1763 John Wilkes, an MP was arrested for writing an inflammatory pamphlet, No. 45, 23 April 1763. In his defence, he continually cited Magna Carta, and the weight that Magna Carta held at the time meant Parliament was wary of continuing the charge. He was released and awarded damages for the wrongful seizure of his papers, as the general warrant under which he was arrested was deemed illegal. He was still expelled from Parliament and spent a week in the Tower of London.

He spent a number of years abroad until 1768 when he returned and failed to be elected as the MP for London. Unperturbed he stood again for Middlesex but he was expelled again based on the earlier offence the next year. He stood again and was elected but the Commons ruled that he was ineligible to sit. At the next three re-elections Wilkes again was the champion, but the House did not relent and his opponent, Lutteral, was announced the winner.

The treatment of Wilkes caused a furore in Parliament, with Lord Camden denouncing the action as a contravention of Magna Carta. Wilkes made the issue a national one and the populace took up the issue. All over the country, there were prints of him being arrested whilst teaching his son about Magna Carta. He received the support of the Corporation of London, which had long sought to establish its supremacy over Parliament, based on the Charter.

Those who supported Wilkes often had little or no knowledge of the actual content of the Charter, or if they did, were looking to protect their own position based on it (such as the Corporation of London). Wilkes re-entered the House in 1774 having begun the cause for a reform movement to 'restore the constitution', through a more representative, less powerful, and shorter termed Parliament.

## Granville Sharp

One of the principal reformists was the philanthropist Granville Sharp. Sharp called for the reform of Parliament based on Magna Carta, and to back this up he devised the doctrine of accumulative authority. This doctrine stated that because almost innumerable parliaments had approved Magna Carta it would take the same number of Parliaments to repeal it. Like many others, Sharp accepted the supremacy of Parliament as an institution, but did not believe that this power was without restraint, and thought that Parliament could not repeal Magna Carta. Many reformists agreed that the Charter was a statement of the liberties of the mythical and immemorial golden age, and there was a popular movement to have a holiday to commemorate the signing of the Charter in a similar way to the American 4th of July holiday; however, very few went as far as Sharp.

## Proposed Reform of Magna Carta

Although there was a popular movement to resist the sovereignty of Parliament based on The Charter, others thought that too much was claimed for the Charter. Cartwright pointed out in 1774 that Magna Carta could not have existed unless there was a firm constitution beforehand. He went even further later and claimed that the Charter was not part of the constitution, but merely a codification of the constitution that existed at the time. Cartwright went on to suggest that there should be a new Magna Carta based on equality and rights for all, not just for landed persons.

People like Cartwright were showing that the rights granted by the Charter were out of pace with the changes that had happened in the intervening six centuries. There were certain provisions, such as Clauses 23 and 39, which were not only still valid then but still form the basis of important rights in the present English law. Undeniably, though, the importance of Magna Carta was diminishing and the arguments for having a fully sovereign Parliament were increasingly accepted. Many in the House still supported the Charter, such as Sir Francis Burdett, who in 1809 called for a return to the constitution of Magna Carta, and denounced the House of Commons for taking proceedings against the radical John Gale Jones, who had accused Parliament of acting in contravention of Magna Carta. Burdett was largely ignored, but he continued, claiming that the Long Parliament (1640-60) had usurped all the power then enjoyed by the Parliament of the time. He stated that Parliament was constantly contravening Magna Carta (although he was referring to its judicial not legislative practice), and that it did not have the right to do so. He received popular support and there were riots across London when he was arrested for these claims.

## Chartists

The major breakthrough occurred in 1828 with the passing of the first Offences Against the Person Act, which for the first time repealed a clause of Magna Carta, namely Clause 36. With the myth broken, in one hundred and fifty years nearly the whole charter was repealed.

The Reform Act 1832 fixed some of the most glaring problems in the political system, but did not go nearly far enough for a group that called itself the Chartists, who called for a return to the constitution of Magna Carta, and eventually created a codification of what they saw as the existing rights of the People, the People's Charter. At a rally for the Chartists in 1838 the Reverend Raynor demanded a return to the constitution of the Charter; freedom of speech, worship and congress. This is a perfect example of how the idea of the Charter went so far beyond its actual content: it depicted for many people the idea of total liberty. It was this over-exaggeration of the Charter that eventually led to its downfall. The more people expected to get from the Charter, the less Parliament was willing to attempt to cater to this expectation, and eventually writers such as Tom Paine refuted the claims about the Charter made by those such as the Chartists. This meant that the educated no longer supported these claims, and the power of Magna Carta as a symbol of freedom gradually faded into obscurity.

## Influences on Later Constitutions

Many later attempts to draft constitutional forms of government, including the United States Constitution, trace their lineage back to this source document. The United States Supreme Court has explicitly referenced Lord Coke's analysis of Magna Carta as an antecedent of the Sixth Amendment's right to a speedy trial.[5]

Magna Carta has influenced international law as well: Eleanor Roosevelt referred to the Universal Declaration of Human Rights as "a Magna Carta for all mankind".

## Jews in England

Magna Carta contained two articles related to money lending and Jews in England. Jewish involvement with money lending caused Christian resentment, because the Church forbade usury; it was seen as vice and was punishable by excommunication, although Jews, as non-Christians, could not be excommunicated and were thus in a legal grey area. Secular leaders, unlike the Church, tolerated the practice of Jewish usury because it gave the leaders opportunity for personal enrichment. This resulted in a complicated legal situation: debtors were frequently trying to bring their Jewish creditors before Church courts, where debts would be absolved as illegal, while the Jews were trying to get their debtors tried in secular courts, where they would be able to collect plus interest. The relations between the debtors and creditors would often become very nasty. There were many attempts over centuries to resolve this problem, and Magna Carta contains one example of the legal code of the time on this issue:

If one who has borrowed from the Jews any sum, great or small, die before that loan be repaid, the debt shall not bear interest while the heir is under age, of whomsoever he may hold; and if the debt fall into our hands, we will not take anything except the principal sum contained in the bond. And if anyone die indebted to the Jews, his wife shall have her dower and pay nothing of that debt; and if any children of the deceased are left under age, necessaries shall be provided for them in keeping with the holding of the deceased; and out of the residue the debt shall be paid, reserving, however, service due to feudal lords; in like manner let it be done touching debts due to others than Jews.

After the Pope annulled Magna Carta, future versions contained no mention of Jews. The Church saw Jews as a threat to their authority, and the welfare of Christians, because of their special relationship to Kings as moneylenders. "Jews are the sponges of kings," wrote the theologian

William de Montibus, "they are bloodsuckers of Christian purses, by whose robbery kings dispoil and deprive poor men of their goods." Thus the specific singling out of Jewish moneylenders seen in Magna Carta originated in part because of Christian nobles who permitted the otherwise illegal activity of usury, a symptom of the larger ongoing power struggle between Church and State during the Middle Ages.

## Popular Perceptions

## Symbol and Practice

Magna Carta is often a symbol for the first time the citizens of England were granted rights against an absolute king. However, in practice the Commons could not enforce Magna Carta in the few situations where it applied to them, so its reach was limited. Also, a large part of Magna Carta was copied, nearly word for word, from the Charter of Liberties of Henry I, issued when Henry I rose to the throne in 1100, which bound the king to laws which effectively granted certain civil liberties to the church and the English nobility.

# Many Documents form the Magna Carta

The document commonly known as Magna Carta today is not the 1215 charter, but a later charter of 1225, and is usually shown in the form of the Charter of 1297 when it was confirmed by Edward I. At the time of the 1215 charter, many of the provisions were not meant to make long-term changes but simply to right some immediate wrongs; therefore, the Charter was reissued three times in the reign of Henry III (1216, 1217 and 1225). After this, each king for the next two hundred years (until Henry V in 1416) personally confirmed the 1225 charter in his own charter. It should not be thought of as one document but rather a variety of documents coming together to form one Magna Carta, in the same way as the treaties of Rome and Nice (among others) come together to form the treaties of the European Union and the European Community.

## The Document was Unsigned

Popular perception is that King John and the barons signed the Magna Carta, however there were no signatures on the original document, only a single seal by the king. The words of the charter-Data per manum nostram-signify that the document was personally given by the king's hand. By placing his seal on the document, the King and the barons followed common law that a seal was sufficient to authenticate a deed, though it had to be done in front of witnesses. John's seal was the only one, and he did not sign it. The barons neither signed nor attached their seals to it.[6]

## America

The document is also honoured in America, where some view it as an antecedent of the United States Constitution and Bill of Rights. The United States has contributed the Runnymede Memorial and Lincoln Cathedral offers a Magna Carta Week.[7] The UK lent one of the four remaining copies of Magna Carta to the U.S. for its bicentennial celebrations and donated a gold copy which is displayed in the U.S. Capitol Rotunda.[8]

## 21st Century Britain

In 2006, BBC History held a poll to recommend a date for a proposed "Britain Day". June 15, as the date of the signing of the original 1215 Magna Carta, received most votes, above other suggestions such as D-Day, VE Day, and Remembrance Day. The outcome was not binding, although the then Chancellor Gordon Brown had previously given his support to the idea of a new national day to celebrate British identity.[9]

## Usage and Spelling

Since there is no direct, consistent correlate of the English definite article in Latin, the usual academic convention is to refer to the document in English without the article as "Magna Carta" rather than "the Magna Carta". According to the Oxford English Dictionary, the first written appearance of the term was in 1218: "Concesserimus libertates quasdam scriptas in magna carta nostra de libertatibus" (Latin: "We concede the certain liberties here written in our great charter of liberties"). However, "the Magna

Carta" is frequently used in both academic and non-academic speech. In the past, the document has also been referred to as "Magna Charta".

## Copies

Numerous copies were made each time it was issued, so all of the participants would each have one — in the case of the 1215 copy, one for the royal archives, one for the Cinque Ports, and one for each of the 40 counties of the time. Several of those copies still exist and some are on permanent display. If there ever was one single 'master copy' of Magna Carta sealed by King John in 1215, it has not survived. Four contemporaneous copies (known as "exemplifications") remain, all of which are located in England:

 * The 'burnt copy', which was found in the records of Dover Castle in the 17th century and so is assumed to be the copy that was sent to the Cinque Ports. It was subsequently involved at a house fire at its owner's property, making it all but illegible. It is the only one of the four to have its seal surviving, although this too was melted out of

shape in the fire. It is currently held by the British Library.

* Another supposedly original, but possibly amended version of the Magna Carta is on show just outside of the chamber of the House of Lords situated in Westminster Palace.

* One owned by Lincoln Cathedral, normally on display at Lincoln Castle. It has an unbroken attested history at Lincoln since 1216. We hear of it in 1800 when the Chapter Clerk of the Cathedral reported that he held it in the Common Chamber, and then nothing until 1846 when the Chapter Clerk of that time moved from within the Cathedral to a property just outside. In 1848, Magna Carta was shown to a visiting group who reported it as "hanging on the wall in an oak frame in beautiful preservation". It went to the New York World Fair in 1939 and so had to be held in Fort Knox, next to the original of the US Constitution, until the end of the Second World War. Having returned to Lincoln, it has been back to America on various occasions since then.[10] It was not on display for a time to undergo conservation in preparation for its visit to

America, where it was exhibited at the Contemporary Art Center of Virginia from March 30 to June 18, 2007 in recognition of the Jamestown quadricentennial.[11][12] From July 4 to July 25, the document was displayed at the National Constitution Center in Philadelphia[13], returning to Lincoln Castle afterwards.

* One owned by and displayed at Salisbury Cathedral. It is the best conserved of the four.

Other early versions of Magna Carta survive. Durham Cathedral possesses 1216, 1217, and 1225 copies.[14]

Four copies are held by the Bodleian Library in Oxford. Three of these are 1217 issues and one a 1225 issue. On 10 Dec 2007, these were put on public display for the first time.[15]

In 1952 the Australian Government purchased a 1297 copy of Magna Carta for £12,500. This copy is now on display in the Members' Hall of Parliament House, Canberra. In January 2006, it was announced by the Department of

Parliamentary Services that the document had been revalued down from A$40m to A$15m.

Only one copy (a 1297 copy with the royal seal of Edward I) is in private hands; it was held by the Brudenell family, earls of Cardigan, who had owned it for five centuries, before being sold to the Perot Foundation in 1984. This copy, having been on long-term loan to the US National Archives, was auctioned at Sotheby's New York on December 18, 2007; The Perot Foundation sold it in order to "have funds available for medical research, for improving public education and for assisting wounded soldiers and their families."[16] It fetched US$21.3 million,[17] It was bought by David Rubenstein of The Carlyle Group,[18] who after the auction said, "I thought it was very important that the Magna Carta stay in the United States and I was concerned that the only copy in the United States might escape as a result of this auction."

## Participant List

Barons, Bishops and Abbots who were party to Magna Carta.[19]

# Barons

Surety Barons for the enforcement of Magna Carta:

* William d'Albini, Lord of Belvoir Castle.
* Roger Bigod, Earl of Norfolk and Suffolk.
* Hugh Bigod, Heir to the Earldoms of Norfolk and Suffolk.
* Henry de Bohun, Earl of Hereford.
* Richard de Clare, Earl of Hertford.
* Gilbert de Clare, heir to the earldom of Hertford.
* John FitzRobert, Lord of Warkworth Castle.
* Robert Fitzwalter, Lord of Dunmow Castle.
* William de Fortibus, Earl of Albemarle.
* William Hardell, **Mayor of the City of London.
* William de Huntingfield, Sheriff of Norfolk and Suffolk.
* John de Lacie, Lord of Pontefract Castle.
* William de Lanvallei, Lord of Standway Castle.
* William Malet, Sheriff of Somerset and Dorset.
* Geoffrey de Mandeville, Earl of Essex and Gloucester.

* William Marshall Jr, heir to the earldom of Pembroke.
* Roger de Montbegon, Lord of Hornby Castle, Lancashire.
* Richard de Montfichet, Baron.
* William de Mowbray, Lord of Axholme Castle.
* Richard de Percy, Baron.
* Saire/Saher de Quincey, Earl of Winchester.
* Robert de Roos, Lord of Hamlake Castle.
* Geoffrey de Saye, Baron.
* Robert de Vere, heir to the earldom of Oxford.
* Eustace de Vesci, Lord of Alnwick Castle.

## Bishops

These bishops being witnesses (mentioned by the King as his advisers in the decision to sign the Charter):

* Stephen Langton, Archbishop of Canterbury, Cardinal of the Holy Roman Church,
* Henry, Archbishop of Dublin
* E. Bishop of London,
* J. Bishop of Bath,
* P. Bishop of Winchester,
* H. Bishop of Lincoln,

* R. Bishop of Salisbury,
* W. Bishop of Rochester,
* W. Bishop of Worcester,
* J. Bishop of Ely,
* H. Bishop of Hereford,
* R. Bishop of Chichester,
* W. Bishop of Exeter.

## Abbots

These abbots being witnesses:

* The Abbot of St. Edmunds
* The Abbot of St. Albans
* The Abbot of Bello
* The Abbot of St. Augustines in Canterbury
* The Abbot of Evesham
* The Abbot of Westminster
* The Abbot of Peterborough
* The Abbot of Reading
* The Abbot of Abingdon
* The Abbot of Malmesbury Abbey
* The Abbot of Winchcomb
* The Abbot of Hyde
* The Abbot of Certesey
* The Abbot of Sherborne

* The Abbot of Cerne
* The Abbot of Abbotebir
* The Abbot of Middleton
* The Abbot of Selby
* The Abbot of Cirencester
* The Abbot of Hartstary

## Others

* Llywelyn the Great Also the other Welsh
Princes
* Master Pandulff, subdeacon and member of the
Papal Household
* Brother Aymeric, Master of the Knights
Templar in England
* Alexander II of Scotland

**For Know-It-Alls**

# Notes

1. (Magna Carta) (1297) (c. 9). UK Statute Law Database. Retrieved on 2007-09-02.

2. by 9 Geo. 4 c. 31 s. 1

3. "Magna Carta". Catholic Encyclopedia. (1913). New York: Robert Appleton Company.

4. http://www.dca.gov.uk/judicial/speeches/lcj150605.htm

5. KLOPFER v. NORTH CAROLINA, 386 U.S. 213 (1967)

6. Browning, Charles Henry (1898). "The Magna Charta Described", The Magna Charta Barons and Their American Descendants..., p. 50. OCLC 9378577.

7. Homepage. Lincoln Cathedral. Retrieved on 2007-09-02. (Select "Visits & Events" > "Magna

Carta" to navigate to the page with this information.)

8. Byrd, Robert (2000-06-15). "Magna Carta" (pdf). Congressional Record — Senate. ISSN 0363-7239. OCLC 2437919. Retrieved on 2006-09-26.

9. "Magna Carta tops British day poll", BBC News, 2006-05-30. Retrieved on 2007-09-02.

10. Knight, Alec (2004-04-17). Magna Charta Our Heritage and Yours. National Society Magna Charta Dames and Barons. Retrieved on 2007-09-02.

11. Magna Carta & Four Foundations of Freedom. Contemporary Art Center of Virginia (2007). Retrieved on 2007-09-02.

12. By Our Heirs Forever. Contemporary Art Center of Virginia (2007). Retrieved on 2007-09-02.

13. National Constitution Center (2007-05-30). "Magna Carta on Display Beginning July 4". Press release. Retrieved on 2007-09-02.

14. Magna Carta: Where Can I See A Copy?. Icons: A Portrait of England. Culture Online. Retrieved on 2007-09-02.

15. Magna Carta on display at the Bodleian (10 December 2007). Retrieved on 2007-12-12.

16. "Magna Carta Is Going on the Auction Block", The New York Times, 25 September 2007. Retrieved on 2007-12-19.

17. "Magna Carta copy fetches $24m", The Sydney Morning Herald, 19 December 2007. Retrieved on 2007-12-19.

18. Magna Carta Sells for $21.3M in New York, Washington Post, 2007-12-19, <http://www.washingtonpost.com/wp-dyn/content/article/2007/12/19/AR2007121900459.html>. Retrieved on 2007-12-19

## 19. Magna Charta translation, Magna Charta Surety Baron Listing, Magna Charta Period Feudal Estates

# References

* "Magna Carta". In Encyclopedia Britannica Online.

* Article from Australia's Parliament House about the relevance of Magna Carta

* J. C. Holt (1992). Magna Carta. Cambridge: Cambridge University Press. ISBN 0-521-27778-7.

* Jennings: Magna Carta and its influence in the world today

* H. Butterfield; Magna Carta in the Historiography of the 16th and 17th Centuries

* G.R.C. Davis; Magna Carta

* J. C. Dickinson; The Great Charter

* G. B. Adams; Constitutional History of England

* A. Pallister; Magna Carta the Legacy of Liberty

* A. Lyon; Constitutional History of the United Kingdom

* G. Williams and J. Ramsden; Ruling Britannia, A Political History of Britain 1688-1988

* Royal letter promulgating the text of Magna Carta (1215), treasure 3 of the British Library displayed via The European Library

# GNU Free Documentation License

Version 1.2, November 2002

## 0. PREAMBLE

The purpose of this License is to make a manual, textbook, or other
functional and useful document "free" in the sense of freedom: to assure
everyone the effective freedom to copy and redistribute it, with or without
modifying it, either commercially or noncommercially. Secondarily, this
License preserves for the author and publisher a way to get credit for their
work, while not being considered responsible for modifications made by
others.

This License is a kind of "copyleft", which means that derivative works of
the document must themselves be free in the same sense. It complements
the GNU General Public License, which is a copyleft license designed for
free software.

We have designed this License in order to use it for manuals for free
software, because free software needs free documentation: a free program
should come with manuals providing the same freedoms that the software
does. But this License is not limited to software manuals; it can be used for
any textual work, regardless of subject matter or whether it is published as a
printed book. We recommend this License principally for works whose
purpose is instruction or reference.

**For Know-It-Alls**


## 1. APPLICABILITY AND DEFINITIONS

This License applies to any manual or other work, in any medium, that contains a notice placed by the copyright holder saying it can be distributed under the terms of this License. Such a notice grants a world-wide, royalty-free license, unlimited in duration, to use that work under the conditions stated herein. The "Document", below, refers to any such manual or work. Any member of the public is a licensee, and is addressed as "you". You accept the license if you copy, modify or distribute the work in a way requiring permission under copyright law.

A "Modified Version" of the Document means any work containing the Document or a portion of it, either copied verbatim, or with modifications and/or translated into another language.

A "Secondary Section" is a named appendix or a front-matter section of the Document that deals exclusively with the relationship of the publishers or authors of the Document to the Document's overall subject (or to related matters) and contains nothing that could fall directly within that overall subject. (Thus, if the Document is in part a textbook of mathematics, a Secondary Section may not explain any mathematics.) The relationship could be a matter of historical connection with the subject or with related matters, or of legal, commercial, philosophical, ethical or political position regarding them.

The "Invariant Sections" are certain Secondary Sections whose titles are designated, as being those of Invariant Sections, in the notice that says that the Document is released under this License. If a section does not fit the above definition of Secondary then it is not allowed to be designated as Invariant. The Document may contain zero Invariant Sections. If the Document does not identify any Invariant Sections then there are none.

The "Cover Texts" are certain short passages of text that are listed, as Front-Cover Texts or Back-Cover Texts, in the notice that says that the Document is released under this License. A Front-Cover Text may be at most 5 words, and a Back-Cover Text may be at most 25 words.

## Magna Carta

A "Transparent" copy of the Document means a machine-readable copy, represented in a format whose specification is available to the general public, that is suitable for revising the document straightforwardly with generic text editors or (for images composed of pixels) generic paint programs or (for drawings) some widely available drawing editor, and that is suitable for input to text formatters or for automatic translation to a variety of formats suitable for input to text formatters. A copy made in an otherwise Transparent file format whose markup, or absence of markup, has been arranged to thwart or discourage subsequent modification by readers is not Transparent. An image format is not Transparent if used for any substantial amount of text. A copy that is not "Transparent" is called "Opaque".

Examples of suitable formats for Transparent copies include plain ASCII without markup, Texinfo input format, LaTeX input format, SGML or XML using a publicly available DTD, and standard-conforming simple HTML, PostScript or PDF designed for human modification. Examples of transparent image formats include PNG, XCF and JPG. Opaque formats include proprietary formats that can be read and edited only by proprietary word processors, SGML or XML for which the DTD and/or processing tools are not generally available, and the machine-generated HTML, PostScript or PDF produced by some word processors for output purposes only.

The "Title Page" means, for a printed book, the title page itself, plus such following pages as are needed to hold, legibly, the material this License requires to appear in the title page. For works in formats which do not have any title page as such, "Title Page" means the text near the most prominent appearance of the work's title, preceding the beginning of the body of the text.

A section "Entitled XYZ" means a named subunit of the Document whose title either is precisely XYZ or contains XYZ in parentheses following text that translates XYZ in another language. (Here XYZ stands for a specific section name mentioned below, such as "Acknowledgements", "Dedications", "Endorsements", or "History".) To "Preserve the Title" of such a section when you modify the Document means that it remains a section "Entitled XYZ" according to this definition.

## For Know-It-Alls

The Document may include Warranty Disclaimers next to the notice which states that this License applies to the Document. These Warranty Disclaimers are considered to be included by reference in this License, but only as regards disclaiming warranties: any other implication that these Warranty Disclaimers may have is void and has no effect on the meaning of this License.

## 2. VERBATIM COPYING

You may copy and distribute the Document in any medium, either commercially or noncommercially, provided that this License, the copyright notices, and the license notice saying this License applies to the Document are reproduced in all copies, and that you add no other conditions whatsoever to those of this License. You may not use technical measures to obstruct or control the reading or further copying of the copies you make or distribute. However, you may accept compensation in exchange for copies. If you distribute a large enough number of copies you must also follow the conditions in section 3.

You may also lend copies, under the same conditions stated above, and you may publicly display copies.

## 3. COPYING IN QUANTITY

If you publish printed copies (or copies in media that commonly have printed covers) of the Document, numbering more than 100, and the Document's license notice requires Cover Texts, you must enclose the copies in covers that carry, clearly and legibly, all these Cover Texts: Front-Cover Texts on the front cover, and Back-Cover Texts on the back cover. Both covers must also clearly and legibly identify you as the publisher of these copies. The front cover must present the full title with all words of the title equally prominent and visible. You may add other material on the covers in addition. Copying with changes limited to the covers, as long as they preserve the title of the Document and satisfy these conditions, can be treated as verbatim copying in other respects.

If the required texts for either cover are too voluminous to fit legibly, you should put the first ones listed (as many as fit reasonably) on the actual cover, and continue the rest onto adjacent pages.

If you publish or distribute Opaque copies of the Document numbering more than 100, you must either include a machine-readable Transparent copy along with each Opaque copy, or state in or with each Opaque copy a computer-network location from which the general network-using public has access to download using public-standard network protocols a complete Transparent copy of the Document, free of added material. If you use the latter option, you must take reasonably prudent steps, when you begin distribution of Opaque copies in quantity, to ensure that this Transparent copy will remain thus accessible at the stated location until at least one year after the last time you distribute an Opaque copy (directly or through your agents or retailers) of that edition to the public.

It is requested, but not required, that you contact the authors of the Document well before redistributing any large number of copies, to give them a chance to provide you with an updated version of the Document.

## 4. MODIFICATIONS

You may copy and distribute a Modified Version of the Document under the conditions of sections 2 and 3 above, provided that you release the Modified Version under precisely this License, with the Modified Version filling the role of the Document, thus licensing distribution and modification of the Modified Version to whoever possesses a copy of it. In addition, you must do these things in the Modified Version:

* A. Use in the Title Page (and on the covers, if any) a title distinct from that of the Document, and from those of previous versions (which should, if there were any, be listed in the History section of the Document). You may use the same title as a previous version if the original publisher of that version gives permission.
* B. List on the Title Page, as authors, one or more persons or entities responsible for authorship of the modifications in the Modified Version, together with at least five of the principal authors of the Document (all of its principal authors, if it has fewer than five), unless they release you from this requirement.
* C. State on the Title page the name of the publisher of the Modified Version, as the publisher.
* D. Preserve all the copyright notices of the Document.

* E. Add an appropriate copyright notice for your modifications adjacent to the other copyright notices.

* F. Include, immediately after the copyright notices, a license notice giving the public permission to use the Modified Version under the terms of this License, in the form shown in the Addendum below.

* G. Preserve in that license notice the full lists of Invariant Sections and required Cover Texts given in the Document's license notice.

* H. Include an unaltered copy of this License.

* I. Preserve the section Entitled "History", Preserve its Title, and add to it an item stating at least the title, year, new authors, and publisher of the Modified Version as given on the Title Page. If there is no section Entitled "History" in the Document, create one stating the title, year, authors, and publisher of the Document as given on its Title Page, then add an item describing the Modified Version as stated in the previous sentence.

* J. Preserve the network location, if any, given in the Document for public access to a Transparent copy of the Document, and likewise the network locations given in the Document for previous versions it was based on. These may be placed in the "History" section. You may omit a network location for a work that was published at least four years before the Document itself, or if the original publisher of the version it refers to gives permission.

* K. For any section Entitled "Acknowledgements" or "Dedications", Preserve the Title of the section, and preserve in the section all the substance and tone of each of the contributor acknowledgements and/or dedications given therein.

* L. Preserve all the Invariant Sections of the Document, unaltered in their text and in their titles. Section numbers or the equivalent are not considered part of the section titles.

* M. Delete any section Entitled "Endorsements". Such a section may not be included in the Modified Version.

* N. Do not retitle any existing section to be Entitled "Endorsements" or to conflict in title with any Invariant Section.

* O. Preserve any Warranty Disclaimers.

If the Modified Version includes new front-matter sections or appendices that qualify as Secondary Sections and contain no material copied from the Document, you may at your option designate some or all of these sections as invariant. To do this, add their titles to the list of Invariant Sections in the

Modified Version's license notice. These titles must be distinct from any other section titles.

You may add a section Entitled "Endorsements", provided it contains nothing but endorsements of your Modified Version by various parties--for example, statements of peer review or that the text has been approved by an organization as the authoritative definition of a standard.

You may add a passage of up to five words as a Front-Cover Text, and a passage of up to 25 words as a Back-Cover Text, to the end of the list of Cover Texts in the Modified Version. Only one passage of Front-Cover Text and one of Back-Cover Text may be added by (or through arrangements made by) any one entity. If the Document already includes a cover text for the same cover, previously added by you or by arrangement made by the same entity you are acting on behalf of, you may not add another; but you may replace the old one, on explicit permission from the previous publisher that added the old one.

The author(s) and publisher(s) of the Document do not by this License give permission to use their names for publicity for or to assert or imply endorsement of any Modified Version.

### 5. COMBINING DOCUMENTS

You may combine the Document with other documents released under this License, under the terms defined in section 4 above for modified versions, provided that you include in the combination all of the Invariant Sections of all of the original documents, unmodified, and list them all as Invariant Sections of your combined work in its license notice, and that you preserve all their Warranty Disclaimers.

The combined work need only contain one copy of this License, and multiple identical Invariant Sections may be replaced with a single copy. If there are multiple Invariant Sections with the same name but different contents, make the title of each such section unique by adding at the end of it, in parentheses, the name of the original author or publisher of that section if known, or else a unique number. Make the same adjustment to the section titles in the list of Invariant Sections in the license notice of the combined work.

In the combination, you must combine any sections Entitled "History" in the various original documents, forming one section Entitled "History"; likewise combine any sections Entitled "Acknowledgements", and any sections Entitled "Dedications". You must delete all sections Entitled "Endorsements."

## 6. COLLECTIONS OF DOCUMENTS

You may make a collection consisting of the Document and other documents released under this License, and replace the individual copies of this License in the various documents with a single copy that is included in the collection, provided that you follow the rules of this License for verbatim copying of each of the documents in all other respects.

You may extract a single document from such a collection, and distribute it individually under this License, provided you insert a copy of this License into the extracted document, and follow this License in all other respects regarding verbatim copying of that document.

## 7. AGGREGATION WITH INDEPENDENT WORKS

A compilation of the Document or its derivatives with other separate and independent documents or works, in or on a volume of a storage or distribution medium, is called an "aggregate" if the copyright resulting from the compilation is not used to limit the legal rights of the compilation's users beyond what the individual works permit. When the Document is included in an aggregate, this License does not apply to the other works in the aggregate which are not themselves derivative works of the Document.

If the Cover Text requirement of section 3 is applicable to these copies of the Document, then if the Document is less than one half of the entire aggregate, the Document's Cover Texts may be placed on covers that bracket the Document within the aggregate, or the electronic equivalent of covers if the Document is in electronic form. Otherwise they must appear on printed covers that bracket the whole aggregate.

## 8. TRANSLATION

Translation is considered a kind of modification, so you may distribute translations of the Document under the terms of section 4. Replacing Invariant Sections with translations requires special permission from their copyright holders, but you may include translations of some or all Invariant Sections in addition to the original versions of these Invariant Sections. You may include a translation of this License, and all the license notices in the Document, and any Warranty Disclaimers, provided that you also include the original English version of this License and the original versions of those notices and disclaimers. In case of a disagreement between the translation and the original version of this License or a notice or disclaimer, the original version will prevail.

If a section in the Document is Entitled "Acknowledgements", "Dedications", or "History", the requirement (section 4) to Preserve its Title (section 1) will typically require changing the actual title.

## 9. TERMINATION

You may not copy, modify, sublicense, or distribute the Document except as expressly provided for under this License. Any other attempt to copy, modify, sublicense or distribute the Document is void, and will automatically terminate your rights under this License. However, parties who have received copies, or rights, from you under this License will not have their licenses terminated so long as such parties remain in full compliance.

## 10. FUTURE REVISIONS OF THIS LICENSE

The Free Software Foundation may publish new, revised versions of the GNU Free Documentation License from time to time. Such new versions will be similar in spirit to the present version, but may differ in detail to address new problems or concerns. See http://www.gnu.org/copyleft/.

Each version of the License is given a distinguishing version number. If the Document specifies that a particular numbered version of this License "or any later version" applies to it, you have the option of following the terms and conditions either of that specified version or of any later version that has been published (not as a draft) by the Free Software Foundation. If the Document does not specify a version number of this License, you may choose any version ever published (not as a draft) by the Free Software Foundation.

How to use this License for your documents

To use this License in a document you have written, include a copy of the License in the document and put the following copyright and license notices just after the title page:

Copyright (c) YEAR YOUR NAME.
Permission is granted to copy, distribute and/or modify this document under the terms of the GNU Free Documentation License, Version 1.2 or any later version published by the Free Software Foundation; with no Invariant Sections, no Front-Cover Texts, and no Back-Cover Texts. A copy of the license is included in the section entitled "GNU
Free Documentation License".

If you have Invariant Sections, Front-Cover Texts and Back-Cover Texts, replace the "with...Texts." line with this:

with the Invariant Sections being LIST THEIR TITLES, with the Front-Cover Texts being LIST, and with the Back-Cover Texts being LIST.

If you have Invariant Sections without Cover Texts, or some other combination of the three, merge those two alternatives to suit the situation.

If your document contains nontrivial examples of program code, we recommend releasing these examples in parallel under your choice of free software license, such as the GNU General Public License, to permit their use in free software.

Lightning Source UK Ltd.
Milton Keynes UK
UKOW06f1320210515

252004UK00013B/208/P